Monetizing Your Music Copyrights and Beyond

Thando Mkize

Published by Thando Mkize, 2024.

MONETIZING YOUR MUSIC COPYRIGHTS AND BEYOND

First edition. September 9, 2024.

ISBN: 979-8227685513

Written by Thando Mkize.

Table of Contents

Introduction 1

Chapter 1: The Basics of Music Copyright 2

Chapter 2: Monetizing Music Copyright 11

Chapter 3: Expanding Beyond Copyright: Additional Revenue Streams 21

Chapter 4: Crafting a Comprehensive International Monetization Plan 29

Chapter 5: Managing and Scaling Your Music Business 37

Chapter 6: The Power of Networking and Building Industry Relationships 46

Chapter 7: Building a Strong Personal Brand in the Music Industry .55

Chapter 8: Mastering Digital Marketing in the Music Industry 64

Chapter 9: Monetizing Your Music Through Streaming and Digital Platforms 75

Chapter 10: Conclusion 86

Introduction

The global music industry is a dynamic and multifaceted arena where creativity meets commerce. For independent artists, songwriters, publishers, record labels, and music entrepreneurs, understanding how to effectively monetize their work is crucial to sustaining a successful career.

This book, "Monetizing Your Music Copyrights and Beyond," is designed to be a comprehensive guide that explores the various ways you can turn your music into a lucrative business. Whether you're just starting out or looking to expand your revenue streams, this book will provide you with the knowledge and tools needed to navigate the complex world of music monetization on a global scale.

In this rapidly evolving industry, having a well-rounded monetization strategy is essential. With the rise of digital platforms, global streaming, and new technologies like blockchain and NFTs, there are more opportunities than ever before to monetize your music. However, understanding how to leverage these opportunities requires a deep knowledge of copyright law, international markets, and the various platforms available for monetizing music.

This book is not just a guide; it's a roadmap to building a sustainable, international music business. By the end of this book, you will have a clear understanding of how to monetize your music copyright, as well as other revenue streams available to you in the modern music industry. More importantly, you will learn how to create a comprehensive monetization plan that can scale globally, ensuring that your music reaches audiences worldwide while maximizing your financial returns.

Let's embark on this journey together, and turn your music into a thriving global business.

Chapter 1: The Basics of Music Copyright

Understanding music copyright is fundamental to successfully monetizing your music and ensuring that you are compensated for your creative work. This chapter will introduce you to the concept of copyright, its significance in the music industry, and the different types of copyrights that apply to music. We'll also explore the role of Collective Management Organizations (CMOs) and key international copyright laws and treaties that protect your rights globally.

1.1 What is Copyright?

Copyright is a legal protection granted to the creators of original works, including music. It gives the creator exclusive rights to use, distribute, and profit from their work. In the context of music, copyright covers both the composition (the melody, harmony, and lyrics) and the recording (the specific performance captured in a sound recording).

When you create an original piece of music, whether it's a song, instrumental piece, or an arrangement, you automatically hold the copyright to that work from the moment it is fixed in a tangible form (e.g., written down or recorded). This means that no one else can legally use, reproduce, or distribute your work without your permission, unless an exception or limitation to copyright law applies.

Key Points:

- Copyright protects original works of authorship, including music.

- It gives the creator exclusive rights to use and distribute their work.

- Copyright is automatically granted once the work is fixed in a tangible form.

1.2 Types of Music Copyright: Composition and Recording

In the music industry, two primary types of copyrights are crucial to understand: the copyright in the composition and the copyright in the recording.

1.2.1 The Copyright in the Composition

The copyright in the composition covers the musical work itself, which includes the melody, harmony, lyrics, and any written or recorded arrangement of these elements. This copyright is typically held by the songwriter or composer, and it can be transferred or licensed to others, such as music publishers or record labels.

The copyright in the composition is often referred to as "publishing rights." These rights are crucial for generating income through various channels, such as mechanical royalties, performance royalties, and synchronization licenses.

Income Streams from the Composition:

- **Mechanical Royalties:** Earned whenever the composition is reproduced or distributed, such as in physical or digital sales.

- **Performance Royalties:** Collected when the composition is performed publicly, whether live or via broadcast.

- **Synchronization Licenses:** Earned when the composition is used in visual media, such as films, TV shows, or commercials.

- **Print Royalties:** Earned when the composition is reproduced into sheet music, or published lyrics (e.g. lyrics displayed on a screen live, or published on a streaming platform, or published in a book).

1.2.2 The Copyright in the Recording

The copyright in the recording, also known as the "master rights," covers the specific sound recording of a performance of the musical work. This is separate from the composition and is typically owned by the entity that financed or used their resources towards the process of creating the record.

Master rights are important for controlling the use of a specific recording. For example, if a song is to be used in a movie or commercial, the license for the master recording must be obtained in addition to the synchronization license for the composition.That is the synchronization license for the recording. If a cover of a song is recorded the master rights of that specific recording belong to the entity(s) who funded the process of recording that master.

Income Streams from the Recording:

- **Mechanical Royalties/Sales:** Earned whenever the record is reproduced or distributed (e.g. sales through digital downloads, or physical CD/vinyl sales)

- **Performance Royalties/Needletime:** Collected when the recording is performed publicly, whether live or via broadcast.

- **Video Play Live (VPL) Royalties:** Collected whenever the music video is performed publicly, whether live or via broadcast.

- **Synchronization Royalties:** Earned when the recording is used in visual media, such as films, TV shows, or commercials.

Examples:

○ **Digital Performance Royalties:** Collected when the recording is streamed or broadcast online (e.g., on platforms like Spotify or Apple Music).

○ **Master Use Licenses:** Must be issued when the specific recording is synced to visual media, such as films or commercials, TV shows or movies.

1.3 The Role of Collective Management Organizations (CMOs)

Collective Management Organizations (CMOs) play a critical role in the music industry by managing the rights of creators and ensuring that they are compensated for the use of their works. These organizations collect and distribute royalties on behalf of songwriters, composers, performers, and record labels.

1.3.1 Types of CMOs

● **Performing Rights Organizations (PROs):** These organizations, such as ASCAP, BMI, and SESAC in the United States, collect performance royalties when a composition is performed publicly. This includes live performances, radio airplay, and broadcasts on TV or the internet.

● **Mechanical Rights Organizations:** Organizations like the Harry Fox Agency (HFA) in the U.S. collect mechanical royalties when a composition is reproduced, such as in CD sales or digital downloads.

- **Neighboring Rights Organizations:** These organizations collect royalties for the public performance of sound recordings. Examples include SoundExchange in the U.S. and PPL in the UK.

1.3.2 How CMOs Operate

CMOs operate by entering into agreements with rightsholders, such as songwriters and publishers, to license their works to users (e.g., radio stations, streaming platforms, retail stores, restaurants, live music venues). They then monitor the usage of these works, collect the corresponding royalties, and distribute them to the rightsholders.

For artists and songwriters, affiliating with CMOs is essential for ensuring that you receive all the royalties you are entitled to, particularly for international performances or broadcasts where it would be difficult to track usage on your own.

Why CMOs Matter:

- They ensure that creators receive royalties for the use of their works.

- CMOs simplify the process of licensing music for various users.

- They provide global reach, ensuring royalty collection across multiple territories.

1.3.3 Reciprocal Agreements Between CMOs

When navigating the complex world of music rights and royalties, it's essential to understand the role of Collective Management Organizations (CMOs) and their reciprocal agreements. CMOs are entities that manage the rights and royalties of creators, including artists, songwriters, publishers, and record labels. These organizations ensure that rights holders are compensated when their music is used commercially, whether in broadcasting, live performances, or digital streaming.

What Are Reciprocal Agreements?

Reciprocal agreements are partnerships between CMOs in different countries or regions that allow them to collect and distribute royalties on behalf of each other's members. For example, if you're a songwriter registered with a CMO in the United States, such as ASCAP or BMI, and your music is played on the radio in France, a French CMO like SACEM will collect the royalties generated from those performances. Through a reciprocal agreement, SACEM then transfers those royalties to your CMO in the U.S., ensuring you receive payment for your work abroad.

Why Are Reciprocal Agreements Important?

These agreements are vital for independent artists and songwriters because they expand the reach of your music beyond your home country without the need to directly engage with multiple CMOs around the world. Essentially, reciprocal agreements allow your music to generate revenue globally, simplifying the process of royalty collection across borders. Without these agreements, you would need to independently register with CMOs in every country where your music is played, which would be time-consuming and costly.

How Can You Benefit?

Understanding how reciprocal agreements work can help you make informed decisions about where to register your copyrights and which CMOs to join. By affiliating with a CMO that has extensive reciprocal agreements, you can maximize your global royalty collection. It's also important to regularly review your CMO's international relationships and make sure they cover the markets where your music is most likely to be played.

For music entrepreneurs managing multiple artists or catalogs, leveraging these agreements is crucial for optimizing revenue streams and ensuring that every possible royalty is captured and distributed accurately. When negotiating contracts or setting up distribution channels, consider how reciprocal agreements might impact your earnings, and ensure that your CMO relationships align with your global ambitions.

In summary, reciprocal agreements between CMOs are a cornerstone of effective international royalty management. By affiliating with the right organizations and understanding the network of agreements in place, you can ensure that your music generates income worldwide, leaving you free to focus on creating and expanding your reach.

1.4 Key International Copyright Laws and Treaties

In today's global music market, understanding international copyright laws and treaties is crucial. These laws ensure that your music is protected and monetized not just in your home country, but across the world.

1.4.1 The Berne Convention

The Berne Convention for the Protection of Literary and Artistic Works is the cornerstone of international copyright law. It ensures that works created in any of its 179 member countries are automatically protected in all other member countries without the need for registration.

Key Features of the Berne Convention:

● **Automatic Protection:** No formalities are required to secure copyright in member countries.

● **Minimum Protection Standards:** Member countries must provide certain minimum protections, such as the right to translation, reproduction, and public performance.

● **Duration of Protection:** Copyright protection must last for at least 50 years after the author's death, although many countries offer longer terms.

1.4.2 The Universal Copyright Convention (UCC)

The UCC is another international agreement that provides an alternative framework for copyright protection, particularly for countries that are not part of the Berne Convention. It ensures that works created in UCC member countries are protected in other member countries.

1.4.3 The WIPO Copyright Treaty (WCT)

The WCT, administered by the World Intellectual Property Organization (WIPO), addresses copyright issues in the digital age. It updates international copyright law to address the challenges and opportunities presented by the internet and digital technologies.

Important Provisions:

● **Digital Rights Management (DRM):** Protection against the circumvention of technological measures used to control access to copyrighted works.

● **Making Available Right:** Authors have the exclusive right to make their works available to the public online.

Conclusion

Understanding the basics of music copyright is the first step towards successfully monetizing your music on a global scale. By securing your rights and understanding the different types of copyright, you can ensure that your creative work is protected and that you are properly compensated for its use. The role of CMOs and the importance of international copyright laws cannot be overstated, as they provide the framework through which your music can generate income across the world.

As you continue to explore the opportunities available in the music industry, remember that a strong foundation in copyright is essential for any successful music career. In the next chapter, we will delve deeper into the various ways you can monetize your music copyright and explore additional revenue streams available to you as an artist, songwriter, publisher, or music entrepreneur.

Chapter 2: Monetizing Music Copyright

Now that you have a solid understanding of music copyright, it's time to explore how you can turn your creative work into a reliable source of income. Monetizing music copyright involves a variety of revenue streams, each with its own set of opportunities and challenges. This chapter will guide you through the primary ways to monetize your music, from collecting royalties to licensing your work for various uses. We'll also cover global royalty collection, digital streaming revenue, and how to maximize your income through strategic partnerships and smart management of your rights.

2.1 Royalties: Mechanical, Performance, and Synchronization

Royalties are one of the most important sources of income for anyone involved in creating music. They represent payments made to rightsholders when their music is used in various ways. Understanding the different types of royalties and how to collect them is crucial for maximizing your earnings.

2.1.1 Mechanical Royalties

Mechanical royalties are earned whenever a musical composition is reproduced in any form. This includes physical copies like CDs and vinyl records, as well as digital formats like downloads and streams. The term "mechanical" originates from the early days of the music industry when compositions were reproduced mechanically, such as through the pressing of vinyl records.

Key Points:

● Mechanical royalties are paid to songwriters and publishers whenever their music is reproduced.

● These royalties are collected by mechanical rights organizations or directly through deals with distributors and record labels.

● Digital service providers (DSPs) like Spotify and Apple Music pay mechanical royalties for each stream or download of a track.

How to Collect Mechanical Royalties:

● **In the U.S.:** The Harry Fox Agency (HFA) is the primary organization responsible for collecting mechanical royalties.

● **Outside the U.S.:** Organizations like MCPS (UK), CAPASSO (South Africa) and others perform similar roles.

● **Direct Licensing**: You can also negotiate direct licenses with labels and distributors.

2.1.2 Performance Royalties

Performance royalties are earned whenever your composition is performed publicly. This can happen in a variety of contexts, such as live concerts, radio broadcasts, streaming services, and even in public spaces like restaurants and shopping centers.

Key Points:

● Performance royalties are collected by Performing Rights Organizations (PROs) on behalf of songwriters and publishers.

● In the U.S., ASCAP, BMI, and SESAC are the primary PROs. Other countries have their own organizations, such as PRS for Music in the UK, and SAMRO in South Africa.

● Live performances, radio airplay, and digital streaming all generate performance royalties.

How to Collect Performance Royalties:

● **Affiliate with a PRO**: Ensure you are registered with a PRO in your country or region.

● **Setlists for Live Performances**: Report your performances to your PRO to collect royalties from live shows.

● **Streaming Services**: Streaming platforms pay performance royalties through your PRO, so ensure your music is properly registered.

2.1.3 Synchronization Royalties

Synchronization (sync) royalties are earned when your music is used in synchronization with visual media, such as films, television shows, advertisements, video games, and online videos. Sync licensing can be particularly lucrative, as the fees for high-profile placements can be substantial.

Key Points:

● Sync royalties are typically paid upfront as a one-time fee when a sync license is granted.

● Both the composition and the recording can generate sync fees, with separate licenses required for each.

● Sync deals often come with additional benefits, such as exposure and promotional opportunities.

How to Collect Synchronization Royalties:

- **Work with a Publisher or Sync Agent**: These professionals can help secure placements in film, TV, and commercials.

- **Direct Licensing**: Some artists choose to handle sync deals themselves, particularly if they own both the composition and the recording.

- **Register Your Music**: Ensure your music is registered with relevant databases, making it easier for media producers to discover and license your work.

2.2 Publishing Agreements: Traditional vs. Self-Publishing

Publishing agreements are contracts between songwriters (or composers) and music publishers. These agreements determine how the income generated by a composition is shared between the songwriter and the publisher. Understanding the different types of publishing deals is crucial for maximizing your earnings and retaining control over your work.

2.2.1 Traditional Publishing

In a traditional publishing deal, a music publisher takes on the responsibility of promoting your compositions and securing licenses. In exchange, the publisher typically receives a percentage of the income generated by the compositions, which is often split 30/70 between the publisher and the songwriter.

Advantages:

• **Promotion and Licensing**: Publishers may actively seek out opportunities to license your music for various uses, including sync placements. This however, is not their core function.

• **Administration**: The core function of Publishers is to handle the administrative work of registering your songs with PROs, and collecting and distributing royalties to their clients. They are also responsible for tracking the usage of their client's music and negotiating synchronization deals on behalf of clients.

Disadvantages:

• **Revenue Split**: You will share a significant portion of your income with the publisher.

• **Creative Control**: In some cases, you may have to give up some control over how your compositions are used.

2.2.2 Self-Publishing

Self-publishing allows you to retain full control over your compositions and collect 100% of the income. However, it also means taking on the responsibility of promoting and administering your music.

Advantages:

• **Full Control**: You retain complete ownership and control over your compositions.

• **Higher Income**: You keep 100% of the income generated by your music.

Disadvantages:

• **Time and Effort**: You will need to handle all aspects of promotion, licensing, and administration yourself.

- **Limited Reach**: Without a publisher's network, it may be more challenging to secure high-profile placements.

Which to Choose?

- **For established artists**: A traditional publishing deal can provide valuable support in maximizing the potential of your compositions.

- **For independent artists**: Self-publishing can be an attractive option, particularly if you are confident in your ability to manage your own business.

2.3 Global Royalty Collection

In today's global music market, it's essential to ensure that your royalties are being collected not just in your home country, but around the world. This can be a complex process, as different countries have different systems for collecting and distributing royalties. However, by affiliating with the right organizations and setting up your global royalty collection strategy, you can ensure that you're getting paid wherever your music is used.

2.3.1 Setting Up with International CMOs

To collect royalties globally, you need to affiliate with CMOs in various territories. While your home country's PRO or mechanical rights organization may have reciprocal agreements with foreign CMOs, it's often beneficial to directly register with key organizations in major markets.

Steps to Take:

- **Research Key Markets**: Identify the countries where your music is likely to be played or used.

- **Register with CMOs**: Affiliate with CMOs in those countries to ensure your royalties are collected.

- **Monitor Your Royalties**: Keep track of your global royalty statements to ensure that all income is being reported and collected.

2.3.2 Reciprocal Agreements

Reciprocal agreements between CMOs allow them to collect royalties on behalf of each other's members. For example, if your music is played in a country where you are not directly affiliated with a CMO, your home CMO may collect those royalties on your behalf.

Benefits:

- **Simplicity**: You don't need to register with every CMO in the world.

- **Broad Coverage**: Reciprocal agreements ensure that you receive royalties from countries where your music is used.

Limitations:

- **Delayed Payments**: It can take longer to receive royalties collected through reciprocal agreements.

- **Administrative Fees**: CMOs may deduct fees for collecting royalties through reciprocal agreements.

2.4 Digital Streaming Revenue

Streaming has become one of the most significant revenue streams for artists in the modern music industry. Platforms like Spotify, Apple Music, and YouTube offer global reach, but understanding how to maximize your income from these platforms requires a strategic approach.

2.4.1 Monetizing Music on Streaming Platforms

Streaming services generate income through both advertising and subscription fees. Artists are paid based on the number of streams their music receives, with the revenue being split between the platform, the rightsholders, and, if applicable, record labels.

Key Points:

● **Per-Stream Payouts**: Streaming payouts are typically low per stream, so building a large audience is key to generating significant income.

● **Rights Management**: Ensure that your music is properly registered with PROs and mechanical rights organizations to collect all applicable royalties.

2.4.2 Strategies for Maximizing Streaming Income

● **Playlist Placements**: Getting your music on popular playlists can significantly boost your streams and visibility.

● **Social Media Promotion**: Use social media platforms to drive traffic to your music on streaming services.

● **Release Strategy**: Regularly releasing new music can help maintain and grow your audience on streaming platforms.

Distribution Services:

● **Digital Aggregators**: Services like DistroKid, TuneCore, and CD Baby can distribute your music to all major streaming platforms, collecting royalties on your behalf.

- **Direct Deals with DSPs**: If you have a significant following, you may be able to negotiate direct deals with streaming platforms, potentially securing higher royalty rates.

2.5 Maximizing Your Income Through Strategic Partnerships

Strategic partnerships can amplify your revenue streams and open up new opportunities for monetization. Whether through licensing deals, brand partnerships, or collaborations with other artists, working with the right partners can help you reach new audiences and maximize your income.

2.5.1 Licensing Deals

Licensing your music for use in films, TV shows, commercials, and video games can provide substantial upfront fees and ongoing royalties. Partnering with sync agents or music supervisors can increase your chances of securing high-profile placements.

2.5.2 Brand Partnerships

Brands are increasingly looking to collaborate with artists to reach new audiences. Partnering with a brand for endorsements, sponsored content, or collaborative projects can be a lucrative revenue stream.

2.5.3 Collaborations

Collaborating with other artists, producers, and songwriters can help you tap into new fan bases and create music that resonates with a broader audience. Collaborations can also lead to co-writing opportunities, resulting in shared royalties.

Conclusion

Monetizing your music copyright involves a multifaceted approach that includes collecting various types of royalties, negotiating publishing deals, ensuring global royalty collection, and maximizing digital streaming revenue. By understanding the different revenue streams available to you and implementing strategies to optimize your income, you can build a sustainable and profitable music career.

In the next chapter, we will explore additional revenue streams beyond copyright monetization, such as live performances, merchandising, and endorsements, to help you further diversify your income and increase your financial stability as a music professional.

Chapter 3: Expanding Beyond Copyright: Additional Revenue Streams

While monetizing music copyright is a crucial aspect of any successful music career, it is by no means the only source of income available to artists, songwriters, publishers, and music entrepreneurs. In this chapter, we will explore additional revenue streams that can significantly enhance your earning potential. These include live performance fees, touring, appearance fees, endorsements, merchandising, and other creative avenues that can supplement and even surpass your income from music royalties.

3.1 Performance Fees: The Heart of Live Music

Live performances are a cornerstone of an artist's career, offering not only a significant revenue stream but also an opportunity to connect with fans and build a loyal audience. Performance fees are payments made to artists for performing live at concerts, festivals, private events, and other venues.

3.1.1 Calculating Performance Fees

Performance fees vary widely depending on factors such as the artist's popularity, the size of the venue, and the event's budget. Established artists can command higher fees, while emerging artists may start with more modest payments.

Key Factors Influencing Performance Fees:

- **Artist's Reputation:** Well-known artists can charge premium fees, while lesser-known acts might need to accept lower fees as they build their careers.

- **Venue Size:** Larger venues with more seating capacity typically offer higher performance fees.

- **Event Type:** Private events and corporate gigs often pay more than standard concert appearances due to the exclusivity and nature of the audience.

Negotiating Performance Fees:

- **Booking Agents:** Many artists work with booking agents who negotiate performance fees on their behalf, ensuring they get the best possible deal.

- **Direct Negotiation:** Independent artists may negotiate directly with venue owners or event organizers, which requires a good understanding of the market rate and the ability to advocate for fair compensation.

3.1.2 Maximizing Income from Live Performances

- **Touring:** By planning and executing tours strategically, artists can maximize their performance fees by booking multiple shows in different cities or countries.

- **Merchandise Sales at Shows:** Selling merchandise at live shows can significantly boost income, as fans are often eager to purchase memorabilia from their favorite artists.

- **Live Recording Releases:** Recording and selling live performances, either as albums or video content, provides another revenue stream while extending the lifespan of the performance.

3.2 Touring: Building a Global Fanbase and Revenue

Touring is an extension of live performances and a vital revenue stream for many artists. Beyond earning performance fees, tours allow artists to reach new audiences, sell merchandise, and build their brand on an international scale.

3.2.1 Planning a Successful Tour

A successful tour requires careful planning and coordination. This includes booking venues, arranging travel and accommodations, and promoting the tour to ensure strong ticket sales.

Steps to Plan a Tour:

● **Select Tour Dates and Locations:** Choose cities and venues that align with your fanbase demographics and where you have the potential to draw large crowds.

● **Budgeting:** Create a budget that accounts for travel, accommodations, crew, production costs, and any other expenses.

● **Sponsorships:** Consider securing sponsorships from brands to offset costs and increase profitability.

3.2.2 Revenue Streams from Touring

● **Performance Fees:** As previously mentioned, performance fees are a primary income source on tour.

● **Merchandise Sales:** Selling tour-specific merchandise can significantly boost income. Limited edition items, exclusive to the tour, tend to sell well.

● **Sponsorship Deals:** Partnering with brands for tour sponsorships can provide additional revenue and help cover costs.

● **VIP Packages:** Offering VIP experiences, such as meet-and-greet sessions, exclusive merchandise, or backstage access, can generate additional income.

3.3 Appearance Fees: Beyond the Stage

In addition to live performances, artists can earn income through appearance fees for attending events, speaking engagements, or participating in media opportunities. Appearance fees are payments made to artists simply for showing up at an event, such as a music festival, a corporate function, or even a product launch.

3.3.1 Opportunities for Earning Appearance Fees

● **Festivals and Award Shows:** Artists often receive appearance fees for attending and participating in music festivals or award ceremonies, especially if they are performing, presenting, or receiving an award.

● **Corporate Events:** Companies may hire artists to make appearances at product launches, company parties, or promotional events.

● **Media Appearances:** Artists can be paid for appearing on television shows, podcasts, or radio interviews, particularly if they are promoting a new release or tour.

Negotiating Appearance Fees:

● **Value Proposition:** The fee is often based on the artist's public profile and the perceived value they bring to the event. High-profile artists can command substantial fees.

- **Inclusions:** Fees can be negotiated to include travel, accommodations, and other expenses, ensuring the artist's comfort and convenience.

3.4 Endorsements: Leveraging Your Brand

Endorsements are another lucrative revenue stream where artists partner with brands to promote products or services. In return, the artist receives a fee, and in some cases, a share of the profits from sales generated by the endorsement.

3.4.1 Types of Endorsement Deals

- **Product Endorsements:** Artists endorse a specific product, often appearing in advertising campaigns or social media promotions.

- **Brand Ambassadorships:** These are longer-term partnerships where the artist becomes a spokesperson for the brand, often involving multiple products or campaigns.

- **Sponsored Content:** Artists create content, such as social media posts or videos, featuring the endorsed product or brand.

Advantages of Endorsements:

- **Significant Income:** Well-negotiated endorsement deals can be extremely profitable, especially with major brands.

- **Brand Alignment:** Associating with reputable brands can enhance an artist's image and reach new audiences.

Challenges:

- **Brand Fit:** It's important for the artist's image and the brand's identity to align, ensuring authenticity in the endorsement.

- **Long-Term Commitments:** Some endorsement deals may require long-term commitments that could limit the artist's ability to work with other brands.

3.5 Merchandising: Turning Fans into Customers

Merchandising is one of the most direct ways to monetize a fanbase. By creating and selling products that resonate with fans, artists can generate significant revenue while enhancing their brand and deepening their connection with their audience.

3.5.1 Types of Merchandise

- **Music Merchandise:** This includes physical music formats like vinyl records, CDs, and cassettes, as well as digital downloads.

- **Apparel:** T-shirts, hoodies, hats, and other clothing items featuring the artist's name, logo, or imagery are perennial bestsellers.

- **Accessories:** Items like posters, stickers, phone cases, and pins offer lower-cost options that appeal to a broad audience.

- **Limited Edition Items:** Exclusive, limited-run products create a sense of urgency and can command higher prices.

3.5.2 Selling Merchandise

- **At Live Shows:** Selling merchandise at concerts and tours is one of the most effective ways to generate sales, as fans are often eager to buy memorabilia.

● **Online Stores:** E-commerce platforms like Shopify, Bandcamp, and Big Cartel allow artists to reach a global audience and sell merchandise directly to fans.

● **Collaborations:** Partnering with fashion brands or designers to create exclusive merchandise can attract a wider audience and add a unique appeal.

Maximizing Merchandise Revenue:

● **Quality Matters:** High-quality products ensure customer satisfaction and can lead to repeat purchases.

● **Marketing and Promotion:** Use social media, email marketing, and live shows to promote new merchandise and special offers.

● **Fan Engagement:** Engage fans in the design process by soliciting their input on new products or offering them limited-edition items.

Conclusion

Diversifying your income streams beyond music copyright is essential for building a sustainable and profitable career in the music industry. By tapping into performance fees, touring, appearance fees, endorsements, and merchandising, artists can create a robust financial foundation that supports their creative endeavors.

Each of these revenue streams offers unique opportunities and challenges, but with careful planning, negotiation, and strategic partnerships, you can maximize your income and grow your music career on a global scale.

In the next chapter, we will explore how to create a comprehensive international monetization plan for your music business. We'll cover strategies for integrating these various revenue streams, optimizing your royalty collection, and expanding your reach through global partnerships and digital platforms.

28

Chapter 4: Crafting a Comprehensive International Monetization Plan

With the foundation of music copyright monetization and additional revenue streams in place, it's time to focus on building a comprehensive international monetization plan. This plan will help you capitalize on every opportunity available in the global music market, ensuring that your music generates income across multiple channels and territories. In this chapter, we will explore strategies for setting up and executing a successful global monetization strategy, including digital distribution, royalty collection, global partnerships, and leveraging digital platforms.

4.1 Establishing Your Global Presence

To monetize your music effectively on an international scale, you need to establish a strong global presence. This involves making your music available in as many markets as possible, partnering with the right organizations, and building a brand that resonates with audiences worldwide.

4.1.1 Digital Distribution

Digital distribution is the cornerstone of global music monetization. By partnering with a digital aggregator, you can ensure that your music is available on streaming platforms, online stores, and other digital outlets around the world.

Choosing a Digital Distributor:

- **Wide Reach:** Select a distributor that provides access to a broad range of platforms, including Spotify, Apple Music, Amazon Music, and regional services like Tencent Music (China) or Anghami (Middle East).

- **Fair Royalties:** Look for a distributor that offers favorable terms, including a high percentage of royalties and transparent reporting.

- **Additional Services:** Some distributors offer marketing, playlist pitching, and royalty collection services, which can enhance your monetization efforts.

Popular Digital Distributors:

- **DistroKid:** Known for its simple pricing model and fast distribution, DistroKid is a popular choice for independent artists.

- **TuneCore:** Offers comprehensive distribution services with detailed analytics and additional monetization options.

- **CD Baby:** Provides a wide range of services, including physical distribution and sync licensing opportunities.

- **OneRPM:** Provides a distribution model with no monthly or yearly subscription fees, where the platform earns a fair percentage of your sales.

4.1.2 International Copyright Registration

To protect your music and ensure you collect all available royalties, it's crucial to register your works with copyright organizations in key markets.

Steps to Register Your Copyright Internationally:

- **U.S. Copyright Office:** Register your works with the U.S. Copyright Office to ensure protection in the U.S. and countries that are members of the Berne Convention.

- **International CMOs:** Register with international collective management organizations (CMOs) in major markets like the UK, Germany, Japan, and Australia.

- **SoundExchange:** Register with SoundExchange to collect digital performance royalties for non-interactive streaming in the U.S.

- **Song Trust:** Register your music with Song Trust and simplify global royalty collection, ensuring you receive all the royalties you're owed from various platforms and territories, even those you may not be aware of.

4.2 Maximizing Global Royalty Collection

To fully monetize your music, you need to ensure that you are collecting all possible royalties from every territory where your music is used. This requires a comprehensive approach to royalty collection that includes both performance and mechanical royalties, as well as digital streaming revenue.

4.2.1 Affiliate with International CMOs

As mentioned in Chapter 2, affiliating with CMOs in key markets is essential for collecting performance and mechanical royalties from around the world.

Steps to Affiliate with International CMOs:

- **Research and Register:** Identify the CMOs in major markets where your music is likely to be used and register your works with them.

- **Reciprocal Agreements:** Take advantage of reciprocal agreements between CMOs to collect royalties from smaller markets without needing to register in every country.

- **Monitor Payments:** Keep a close eye on your royalty statements to ensure you are receiving payments from all relevant territories.

4.2.2 Digital Streaming Royalties

Streaming platforms are a major source of income for artists in today's music industry. To maximize your streaming revenue, you need to ensure that your music is available on all major platforms and that you are collecting all applicable royalties.

Key Strategies for Maximizing Streaming Royalties:

- **Global Distribution:** Ensure your music is available on all major streaming platforms in every market, including region-specific services.

- **Optimize Metadata:** Properly tag and register your music with all relevant data (songwriter credits, ISRC codes, etc.) to ensure accurate royalty payments.

- **Promote Globally:** Use social media, digital marketing, and playlist pitching to promote your music to audiences around the world.

4.3 Leveraging Global Partnerships

Building partnerships with key players in the global music industry can significantly enhance your ability to monetize your music on an international scale. These partnerships can include working with international labels, publishers, sync agents, and brands.

MONETIZING YOUR MUSIC COPYRIGHTS AND BEYOND

4.3.1 Partnering with International Labels

While many independent artists prefer to retain full control over their music, partnering with an international label can provide valuable resources and exposure in new markets.

Benefits of Label Partnerships:

• **Global Distribution:** Labels often have established distribution networks that can ensure your music reaches new markets.

• **Marketing Support:** Labels can provide marketing and promotional support, helping to increase your visibility and audience reach.

• **Touring and Live Events:** Labels can assist with organizing international tours and securing high-profile live performance opportunities.

4.3.2 Working with Global Publishers

If you choose to work with a music publisher, selecting one with a strong international presence can open up new opportunities for licensing and synchronization deals.

Advantages of Global Publishing Deals:

• **Sync Licensing:** Global publishers have connections with film, TV, and advertising industries around the world, increasing your chances of landing lucrative sync deals.

• **Co-Writing Opportunities:** Publishers can facilitate collaborations with international songwriters, leading to new creative opportunities and revenue streams.

- **Administration:** Publishers handle the administrative tasks of registering your works and collecting royalties, ensuring you receive payments from all applicable territories.

4.4 Expanding Your Reach with Digital Platforms

In the digital age, online platforms offer unparalleled opportunities to expand your reach and monetize your music on a global scale. By leveraging social media, video platforms, and direct-to-fan sales, you can build a global fanbase and create new revenue streams.

MONETIZING YOUR MUSIC COPYRIGHTS AND BEYOND

4.4.1 Social Media and Content Platforms

Social media platforms like Instagram, TikTok, and Twitter are essential tools for building and engaging with a global audience. Additionally, video platforms like YouTube offer opportunities to monetize your content through ad revenue and fan support.

Strategies for Expanding Your Reach:

● **Consistent Content:** Regularly post engaging content to maintain and grow your audience. This can include music videos, behind-the-scenes footage, live streams, and fan interactions.

● **Global Campaigns:** Create social media campaigns that resonate with audiences in different regions, taking cultural differences into account.

● **Monetization Tools:** Use monetization tools available on platforms like YouTube (e.g., ad revenue, Super Chats, memberships) and Instagram (e.g., sponsored posts, fan badges) to generate income.

4.4.2 Direct-to-Fan Sales

Selling directly to your fans through platforms like Bandcamp, Patreon, or your own website allows you to retain more of the revenue and build a closer relationship with your audience.

Benefits of Direct-to-Fan Sales:

● **Higher Margins:** By selling directly, you avoid the fees and revenue splits associated with third-party platforms.

● **Exclusive Content:** Offer fans exclusive content, such as early access to new music, limited edition merchandise, or VIP experiences.

● **Crowdfunding:** Platforms like Patreon allow fans to support your work on a recurring basis, providing a steady income stream.

Conclusion

Creating a comprehensive international monetization plan is essential for maximizing your income and sustaining a successful career in the global music industry. By establishing a global presence, maximizing royalty collection, building strategic partnerships, and leveraging digital platforms, you can ensure that your music reaches its full potential and generates income across multiple channels and territories.

In the next chapter, we will explore how to manage and scale your music business effectively, covering topics such as financial management, team building, and long-term strategic planning to support your growth and success in the competitive music industry.

Chapter 5: Managing and Scaling Your Music Business

As your music career begins to grow and your income streams diversify, it becomes increasingly important to manage your business effectively and plan for long-term success. In this chapter, we will explore key strategies for managing and scaling your music business, including financial management, building a strong team, strategic planning, and leveraging technology to streamline operations.

5.1 Financial Management: Building a Solid Foundation

Effective financial management is the backbone of any successful business, and the music industry is no exception. As your income grows, you'll need to implement sound financial practices to manage your revenue, control expenses, and plan for the future.

5.1.1 Budgeting and Cash Flow Management

Creating and maintaining a budget is essential for tracking your income and expenses, ensuring that your business remains financially stable.

Key Steps in Budgeting:

● **Estimate Income:** Project your expected revenue from various sources, including royalties, live performances, merchandise sales, and endorsements.

● **Track Expenses:** Record all business expenses, including production costs, marketing, touring expenses, and professional fees (e.g., lawyers, accountants).

- **Manage Cash Flow:** Ensure that your income is sufficient to cover your expenses, particularly during periods of lower revenue (e.g., between tours or album releases).

Tools for Budgeting and Cash Flow:

- **Accounting Software:** Use tools like QuickBooks, Xero, or Wave to manage your finances, track expenses, and generate financial reports.

- **Financial Advisors:** Consider hiring a financial advisor or accountant with experience in the music industry to help you manage your finances effectively.

5.1.2 Tax Planning and Compliance

As your music business grows, you'll need to navigate the complexities of tax planning and compliance, both domestically and internationally.

Key Tax Considerations:

● **Income Tax:** Ensure that you report all income accurately and take advantage of any available deductions related to your music business.

● **Sales Tax:** If you're selling merchandise, tickets, or other products, you may be required to collect and remit sales tax, depending on your location.

● **International Taxation:** If you're earning income from multiple countries, you may need to navigate international tax laws and treaties to avoid double taxation.

Working with a Tax Professional:

● **Specialized Expertise:** Consider working with a tax professional who understands the unique challenges of the music industry, particularly if you have income from multiple jurisdictions.

● **Tax Planning:** Engage in proactive tax planning to minimize your tax liability and ensure compliance with all relevant regulations.

5.2 Building a Strong Team: Collaborating for Success

As your career progresses, you'll need to build a team of professionals to support your business operations, allowing you to focus on your creative work. A strong team can help you manage the various aspects of your music business, from legal matters to marketing and beyond.

5.2.1 Key Roles in Your Music Business

There are several key roles that can contribute to the success of your music business. Depending on your needs and resources, you may choose to hire full-time staff, work with freelancers, or engage with third-party agencies.

Essential Team Members:

● **Manager:** A manager oversees your career, helping to make strategic decisions, secure opportunities, and manage your day-to-day business operations.

● **Booking Agent:** A booking agent is responsible for securing live performance opportunities, including concerts, tours, and festival appearances.

● **Publicist:** A publicist manages your public image and media relations, securing press coverage, interviews, and other promotional opportunities.

● **Lawyer:** A music lawyer handles legal matters, including contracts, intellectual property protection, and dispute resolution.

● **Accountant/Financial Advisor:** A financial professional helps manage your finances, including budgeting, tax planning, and investment strategies.

● **Social Media Manager:** This role involves managing your online presence, engaging with fans, and promoting your music on social media platforms.

Alternative Team Member

Music Business Consultant: A music business consultant can be a versatile addition to your essential team, providing strategic guidance across multiple areas like career management, legal advice, and social media strategy. By offering a holistic view of your business, they can often substitute traditional roles such as a manager, lawyer, or social media manager, streamlining your operations and ensuring cohesive decision-making.

5.2.2 Building and Managing Your Team

Once you've identified the key roles needed for your business, the next step is to find the right people and manage your team effectively.

Finding the Right Talent:

● **Networking:** Leverage industry connections and attend events to meet potential team members and collaborators.

● **Referrals:** Ask for recommendations from trusted colleagues and industry professionals.

● **Hiring Platforms:** Use platforms like LinkedIn, Music Jobs, or specialized music industry job boards to find qualified candidates.

Managing Your Team:

● **Clear Communication:** Establish open lines of communication and set clear expectations for each team member's role and responsibilities.

● **Performance Reviews:** Regularly assess the performance of your team members and provide feedback to ensure that everyone is aligned with your goals.

● **Collaboration:** Foster a collaborative environment where team members work together to achieve your business objectives.

5.3 Strategic Planning: Setting Goals for Long-Term Success

Strategic planning is essential for ensuring the long-term growth and sustainability of your music business. By setting clear goals and developing a roadmap to achieve them, you can navigate the challenges of the music industry and capitalize on new opportunities.

5.3.1 Setting SMART Goals

SMART goals are Specific, Measurable, Achievable, Relevant, and Time-bound. Setting SMART goals for your music business can help you stay focused and measure your progress over time.

Examples of SMART Goals:

● **Increase Streaming Revenue:** "Increase streaming revenue by 20% within the next 12 months by improving playlist placement and expanding to new platforms."

● **Expand International Presence:** "Secure distribution deals in three new countries by the end of the year to increase global reach."

● **Release New Music:** "Release two EPs and one full-length album over the next 18 months, with supporting marketing and promotion strategies."

5.3.2 Creating a Strategic Plan

Once you've set your goals, the next step is to create a strategic plan that outlines the actions you'll take to achieve them.

Steps in Strategic Planning:

● **Conduct a SWOT Analysis:** Assess your business's Strengths, Weaknesses, Opportunities, and Threats to inform your strategy.

- **Develop Action Plans:** For each goal, create a detailed action plan that outlines the steps needed to achieve it, along with timelines and resources required.

- **Monitor and Adjust:** Regularly review your strategic plan and adjust your tactics as needed based on market conditions and business performance.

5.4 Leveraging Technology for Growth

In today's digital landscape, technology plays a crucial role in the growth and scalability of your music business. By leveraging the right tools and platforms, you can streamline operations, reach a wider audience, and optimize your business processes.

5.4.1 Digital Tools for Business Management

There are numerous digital tools available to help you manage different aspects of your music business, from project management to marketing and beyond.

Key Tools and Platforms:

- **Project Management:** Tools like Asana, Trello, or Monday.com can help you manage tasks, collaborate with your team, and keep track of deadlines.

- **Marketing Automation:** Platforms like Mailchimp, HubSpot, or Hootsuite can automate your marketing efforts, including email campaigns, social media posts, and audience engagement.

- **Financial Management:** As mentioned earlier, accounting software like QuickBooks or Xero can help you manage your finances, track expenses, and generate reports.

• **Data Analytics:** Use analytics tools provided by streaming platforms, social media, and your own website to gain insights into your audience's behavior and preferences, guiding your marketing and content strategies.

5.4.2 Scaling Your Business with Technology

As your music business grows, technology can help you scale your operations efficiently, allowing you to reach more fans, generate more revenue, and expand your business globally.

Strategies for Scaling with Technology:

• **E-Commerce:** Set up an online store to sell music, merchandise, and exclusive content directly to fans, using platforms like Shopify, Bandcamp, or WooCommerce.

• **Digital Marketing:** Use targeted digital marketing campaigns to reach new audiences and promote your music on a global scale.

• **Streaming Optimization:** Use data from streaming platforms to optimize your release strategies, improve playlist placement, and increase streaming revenue.

• **Automation:** Automate routine tasks like social media posting, email marketing, and financial reporting to free up time for creative and strategic work.

Conclusion

Managing and scaling your music business requires a combination of strategic planning, effective financial management, a strong team, and the right technology. By building a solid foundation in these areas, you can ensure the long-term success and sustainability of your music career.

As you continue to grow and evolve as an artist and entrepreneur, remember that the music industry is constantly changing. Stay adaptable, continue learning, and be open to new opportunities that can help you achieve your goals and reach new heights in your career.

In the next chapter, we will delve into the importance of networking and building relationships within the music industry. We'll explore how to create a powerful network of contacts, leverage industry connections, and collaborate with others to advance your career and business.

Chapter 6: The Power of Networking and Building Industry Relationships

In the music industry, who you know can often be as important as what you know. Building strong relationships and networking effectively can open doors to new opportunities, collaborations, and resources that can propel your career to the next level. In this chapter, we will explore the importance of networking, strategies for building and maintaining industry relationships, and how to leverage your network to achieve your business goals.

6.1 The Importance of Networking in the Music Industry

Networking is more than just exchanging business cards or adding contacts on social media. It's about building meaningful relationships that can provide mutual benefits, whether through collaborations, opportunities, or shared knowledge.

6.1.1 Why Networking Matters

In an industry as interconnected as music, networking plays a crucial role in your success for several reasons:

- **Access to Opportunities:** Many opportunities in the music industry are never advertised publicly. They come through personal connections, word-of-mouth, and recommendations. A strong network increases your chances of being considered for these opportunities.

• **Collaboration:** Networking helps you find like-minded individuals with whom you can collaborate, whether on songwriting, production, or other creative projects.

• **Learning and Growth:** By connecting with others in the industry, you can gain valuable insights, learn from their experiences, and stay informed about industry trends and best practices.

• **Support System:** The music industry can be challenging and having a network of peers and mentors can provide support, guidance, and encouragement when you need it.

6.1.2 The Types of Relationships to Build

Different types of relationships can provide different benefits to your music career. Here are some key types of connections to focus on:

• **Peers:** Fellow musicians, songwriters, and producers who are at a similar stage in their careers can offer support, collaboration opportunities, and shared experiences.

• **Mentors:** Experienced industry professionals who can provide guidance, advice, and introductions to key players in the industry.

• **Industry Professionals:** Agents, managers, publicists, and other professionals who can help manage and promote your career.

• **Fans and Supporters:** Building a strong relationship with your fans is essential for your long-term success. Engaged fans can become your best promoters and advocates.

• **Business Contacts:** These include venue owners, festival organizers, label executives, and other decision-makers who can provide opportunities for performances, deals, and other career advancements.

6.2 Strategies for Building a Strong Network

Building a strong network requires more than just attending events or sending connection requests. It involves actively engaging with people, offering value, and nurturing relationships over time.

6.2.1 Attending Industry Events

Industry events such as conferences, festivals, workshops, and networking mixers are prime opportunities to meet new people and expand your network.

Tips for Networking at Events:

● **Be Prepared:** Have a clear idea of what you want to achieve at the event. Whether it's meeting a specific person or learning about a particular topic, having a goal will help you stay focused.

● **Elevator Pitch:** Prepare a concise, compelling description of who you are and what you do. This will help you introduce yourself effectively to new contacts.

● **Be Approachable:** Smile, make eye contact, and be open to conversations. Networking is as much about listening as it is about talking.

● **Follow Up:** After the event, follow up with the people you met. Send a friendly email or message to keep the conversation going and explore potential opportunities to work together.

6.2.2 Leveraging Social Media for Networking

Social media platforms like LinkedIn, Instagram, Twitter, and Facebook are powerful tools for networking in the digital age. They allow you to connect with people from around the world and build relationships without geographical constraints.

Effective Social Media Networking Strategies:

• **Engage with Content:** Regularly like, comment, and share posts from people in your network. This shows that you're active and interested in what they're doing.

• **Join Industry Groups:** Participate in online groups, forums, and communities related to the music industry. Engage in discussions, share your insights, and connect with other members.

• **Share Valuable Content:** Post content that showcases your expertise, whether it's your latest music release, industry insights, or behind-the-scenes glimpses of your creative process. This helps establish your authority and keeps your network engaged.

• **Direct Outreach:** Don't be afraid to reach out to people you admire or want to connect with. Send a personalized message introducing yourself and explaining why you'd like to connect.

6.2.3 Building Relationships with Industry Gatekeepers

Industry gatekeepers, such as A&R representatives, booking agents, and label executives, can play a significant role in your career. Building relationships with these key players can help you access opportunities that might otherwise be out of reach.

Approaching Industry Gatekeepers:

• **Research:** Before reaching out, research the person you want to connect with. Understand their role, what they've worked on, and how you might align with their interests.

- **Offer Value:** Instead of asking for something right away, think about how you can offer value to the relationship. This could be as simple as sharing useful information or offering to collaborate on a project.

- **Be Patient and Persistent:** Building relationships with gatekeepers takes time. Be patient, follow up respectfully, and continue to build your relationship over time.

6.3 Maintaining and Nurturing Relationships

Building a network is just the first step. Maintaining and nurturing your relationships over time is what turns a network into a valuable resource.

6.3.1 Staying in Touch

Regular communication is key to maintaining strong relationships. Stay in touch with your contacts, even when you don't have a specific reason to reach out.

Ways to Stay Connected:

- **Check-Ins:** Periodically check in with your contacts to see how they're doing and update them on your latest projects.

- **Share Opportunities:** If you come across opportunities that might be of interest to someone in your network, share them. This shows that you're thinking of them and are invested in their success.

- **Invite Collaboration:** Look for opportunities to collaborate with people in your network. Whether it's a co-writing session, a joint performance, or a shared promotional campaign, collaboration helps strengthen relationships.

6.3.2 Offering Value Consistently

One of the best ways to nurture relationships is by consistently offering value. This could be in the form of sharing your expertise, providing introductions, or offering support when needed.

Ways to Offer Value:

• **Provide Insights:** Share your knowledge and insights on industry trends, opportunities, or best practices that might benefit your contacts.

• **Be a Connector:** Introduce people in your network who might benefit from knowing each other. Being a connector helps you build goodwill and strengthens your network.

• **Support Their Work:** Attend their events, promote their projects, or offer constructive feedback. Showing support for others helps build trust and reciprocity.

6.4 Leveraging Your Network for Business Growth

Once you've built and nurtured your network, the next step is to leverage it for your business growth. A strong network can open doors to new opportunities, collaborations, and partnerships that can accelerate your career.

6.4.1 Finding Collaboration Opportunities

Collaboration is one of the most powerful ways to leverage your network. Whether it's co-writing a song, producing a track, or planning a joint tour, collaborations can help you reach new audiences and expand your creative horizons.

Identifying Collaboration Opportunities:

- **Complementary Skills:** Look for people in your network who have skills or expertise that complement your own. This can lead to more innovative and successful collaborations.

- **Shared Goals:** Collaborate with people who share similar goals or values. This alignment can lead to more productive and satisfying partnerships.

- **Cross-Promotion:** Partner with other artists or industry professionals to cross-promote each other's work. This can help both parties reach new audiences and build their brands.

6.4.2 Securing Opportunities Through Referrals

Referrals are a powerful way to secure new opportunities in the music industry. When someone in your network recommends you for a project or opportunity, it carries more weight than a cold approach.

How to Encourage Referrals:

● **Build Trust:** Ensure that you're reliable, professional, and deliver high-quality work. People are more likely to refer you if they trust that you'll make them look good.

● **Ask for Referrals:** Don't be afraid to ask for referrals from people you have a strong relationship with. Let them know the type of opportunities you're looking for and ask if they can recommend you.

● **Reciprocate:** Be willing to refer others when appropriate. Reciprocity strengthens relationships and encourages others to do the same for you.

6.4.3 Expanding Your Business Through Partnerships

Partnerships with other artists, brands, or businesses can help you scale your music business and reach new markets. These partnerships can take many forms, from joint ventures to brand endorsements.

Exploring Partnership Opportunities:

● **Brand Collaborations:** Partner with brands that align with your image and values. Brand collaborations can provide additional revenue streams and increase your visibility.

● **Joint Ventures:** Consider forming joint ventures with other artists or businesses to co-create products, launch tours, or develop new markets.

● **Strategic Alliances:** Form strategic alliances with companies that offer complementary services, such as music production, distribution, or marketing. These alliances can help you grow your business more efficiently.

Conclusion

Networking and building strong industry relationships are essential components of a successful music career. By actively engaging with others in the industry, offering value, and nurturing your relationships over time, you can create a powerful network that supports your growth and opens doors to new opportunities.

As you continue to build your career, remember that networking is an ongoing process. Stay proactive in maintaining your relationships, seek out new connections, and be open to collaborations and partnerships that can help you achieve your business goals.

In the next chapter, we will explore the role of branding in the music industry. We'll discuss how to create a strong personal brand, develop a consistent image, and use branding to differentiate yourself in a crowded market.

Chapter 7: Building a Strong Personal Brand in the Music Industry

In the modern music industry, branding is as important as your musical talent. A strong personal brand not only differentiates you from other artists but also creates a lasting impression that resonates with fans, industry professionals, and potential collaborators. In this chapter, we will explore the importance of personal branding, the steps to create a compelling brand, and how to maintain and evolve your brand as your career progresses.

7.1 The Importance of Personal Branding

A personal brand is the unique combination of your identity, values, image, and the way you communicate with your audience. It reflects who you are as an artist and helps you stand out in a crowded and competitive industry.

7.1.1 Why Branding Matters

Branding is essential for several reasons:

- **Recognition:** A strong brand makes you recognizable and memorable to your audience. It helps fans identify and connect with you across various platforms and mediums.

- **Connection:** Your brand allows you to build a deeper emotional connection with your fans. When your audience resonates with your brand's story, values, and message, they are more likely to become loyal supporters.

• **Differentiation:** In a saturated market, branding sets you apart from other artists. It highlights what makes you unique and why people should pay attention to your music.

• **Commercial Success:** A well-defined brand can open doors to more opportunities, including endorsements, partnerships, and higher sales of music and merchandise.

7.1.2 The Elements of a Personal Brand

Your personal brand is made up of several key elements that work together to create a cohesive and compelling image:

• **Visual Identity:** This includes your logo, color scheme, typography, album artwork, and overall aesthetic. Your visual identity should be consistent across all your platforms.

• **Voice and Tone:** Your brand's voice and tone refer to how you communicate with your audience. Are you formal or casual, humorous or serious, inspiring or rebellious? Consistency in your voice helps build trust and familiarity.

• **Values and Mission:** Your core values and mission define what you stand for as an artist. This could be your commitment to authenticity, social justice, creativity, or any other principles that guide your work.

• **Story and Narrative:** Your story is a powerful tool for building a brand. It could include your background, struggles, triumphs, and the journey that has led you to where you are today. A compelling narrative helps fans relate to you on a personal level.

• **Target Audience:** Understanding who your audience is and what they care about is crucial for building a brand that resonates. Your brand should speak directly to your audience's needs, desires, and emotions.

7.2 Crafting Your Personal Brand

Building a strong personal brand requires intentionality and strategic planning. It's about defining who you are, what you stand for, and how you want to be perceived by the world.

7.2.1 Defining Your Brand Identity

The first step in building your brand is to define your brand identity. This involves a deep understanding of your unique qualities, values, and goals.

Steps to Define Your Brand Identity:

• **Self-Reflection:** Start by reflecting on your journey as an artist. What are your core values? What message do you want to convey through your music? What sets you apart from other artists?

• **Identify Your Strengths:** Determine the key strengths that you bring to the table. This could be your musical style, lyrical content, performance energy, or visual creativity.

• **Clarify Your Mission:** Define your mission as an artist. What do you hope to achieve with your music? How do you want to impact your audience and the world?

• **Understand Your Audience:** Identify who your target audience is. What are their demographics, interests, and values? How can you connect with them on a deeper level?

7.2.2 Creating a Visual and Verbal Identity

Once you've defined your brand identity, the next step is to create a visual and verbal identity that aligns with your brand.

Developing a Visual Identity:

● **Logo:** Design a logo that represents your brand. It should be simple, memorable, and versatile enough to be used across various platforms.

● **Color Palette:** Choose a color palette that reflects your brand's personality. Colors evoke emotions and can reinforce the tone of your brand.

● **Typography:** Select fonts that complement your brand's style and are consistent across all your materials, including album covers, websites, and promotional materials.

● **Photography and Imagery:** Use consistent photography and imagery that align with your brand's aesthetic. This includes album covers, promotional photos, and social media content.

Crafting a Verbal Identity:

● **Voice:** Define the tone and style of your communication. Are you conversational, poetic, edgy, or inspirational? Your voice should be consistent across all your communications, from social media posts to interviews.

● **Messaging:** Create key messages that encapsulate your brand's values and mission. These should be clear, concise, and reflect what you want your audience to know about you.

● **Taglines and Slogans:** Develop a tagline or slogan that captures the essence of your brand. This should be memorable and encapsulate your brand's core message.

7.2.3 Developing a Brand Narrative

Your brand narrative is the story you tell about yourself as an artist. It's how you connect with your audience on an emotional level and convey the journey that has shaped your music.

Crafting Your Brand Narrative:

● **Your Background:** Share your origins—where you come from, how you started in music, and what inspired you to pursue this path.

● **Challenges and Triumphs:** Highlight the challenges you've faced and the triumphs you've achieved. This adds depth to your story and makes it relatable.

● **Vision for the Future:** Talk about your goals and aspirations. What do you hope to achieve in the future? How will your journey continue to evolve?

7.3 Communicating Your Brand to the World

Once you've crafted your brand, the next step is to communicate it consistently across all channels. This includes your online presence, social media, live performances, and media interactions.

7.3.1 Online Presence and Social Media

Your online presence is the primary way your audience interacts with your brand. It's essential to ensure that your branding is consistent across all your digital platforms.

Building a Strong Online Presence:

- **Website:** Your website is your digital home base. It should reflect your brand's visual and verbal identity and provide a hub for all your content, including music, videos, tour dates, and merchandise.

- **Social Media Profiles:** Ensure that your branding is consistent across all your social media profiles. This includes using the same profile picture, bio, and branding elements.

- **Content Strategy:** Develop a content strategy that aligns with your brand's voice and values. This could include behind-the-scenes content, storytelling posts, live streams, and fan interactions.

- **Engagement:** Actively engage with your audience on social media. Respond to comments, participate in conversations, and create content that encourages interaction.

7.3.2 Live Performances and Public Appearances

Your live performances and public appearances are opportunities to reinforce your brand and connect with your audience in a personal way.

Branding Through Live Performances:

- **Stage Presence:** Your stage presence should reflect your brand's personality. Whether you're high-energy, soulful, or introspective, ensure that your performance style is consistent with your brand.

- **Visual Elements:** Incorporate branding elements into your stage design, lighting, and costumes. This creates a cohesive experience for your audience.

- **Audience Interaction:** How you interact with your audience during performances can reinforce your brand. Consider how you address the crowd, introduce songs, and engage with fans during and after the show.

7.3.3 Media and Public Relations

Media coverage and public relations play a significant role in shaping public perception of your brand. How you handle interviews, press releases, and media interactions can impact your brand's reputation.

Managing Media Relations:

● **Press Kit:** Create a professional press kit that includes your bio, photos, music samples, and key messages. This should be consistent with your brand identity and ready to share with media outlets.

● **Interviews:** Prepare for interviews by aligning your responses with your brand's messaging. Be authentic and consistent in how you present yourself.

● **Publicity Campaigns:** Work with publicists or PR professionals to develop campaigns that highlight your brand's unique qualities and create buzz around your music.

7.4 Evolving Your Brand

As your career progresses, your brand may need to evolve. This could be in response to changes in your music style, personal growth, or shifts in the industry. Evolving your brand while maintaining its core essence is crucial for long-term success.

7.4.1 Recognizing When to Evolve

There are several signs that it may be time to evolve your brand:

● **Change in Music Style:** If your music style has significantly changed, your brand may need to be updated to reflect this new direction.

● **New Audience:** As you grow, you may attract a new audience with different expectations and preferences. Your brand should evolve to resonate with this new demographic.

● **Personal Growth:** Your brand should reflect who you are. As you grow and change as a person, your brand may need to be updated to stay authentic.

7.4.2 Evolving Without Losing Your Core Identity

When evolving your brand, it's essential to maintain the core elements that make you unique. This ensures continuity and helps retain your existing fan base.

Steps to Evolve Your Brand:

● **Reassess Your Identity:** Reflect on your current brand identity and how it aligns with who you are today. Identify the core elements that should remain unchanged.

● **Update Visuals and Messaging:** Refresh your visual and verbal identity to reflect the evolution of your brand. This could include updating your logo, color palette, messaging, and website design.

● **Communicate the Change:** Be transparent with your audience about the changes to your brand. Share the story behind the evolution and how it reflects your growth as an artist.

● **Test and Iterate:** As you evolve your brand, test how your audience responds to the changes. Be open to feedback and make adjustments as needed.

Conclusion

Building a strong personal brand is a critical component of success in the music industry. Your brand is your identity, your story, and your promise to your audience. By crafting a compelling brand, communicating it consistently, and evolving it as you grow, you can create a lasting impression that resonates with fans and industry professionals alike.

In the next chapter, we will delve into the world of digital marketing for musicians. We'll explore how to create effective marketing campaigns, build a strong online presence, and leverage digital tools to grow your fan base and monetize your music.

Chapter 8: Mastering Digital Marketing in the Music Industry

Digital marketing is an essential tool for independent artists, songwriters, publishers, record labels, and music entrepreneurs. It's how you reach new audiences, engage with fans, and ultimately, monetize your music in the digital age. In this chapter, we will explore the key components of a successful digital marketing strategy, including building a strong online presence, leveraging social media, using email marketing, and understanding analytics to optimize your efforts.

8.1 The Fundamentals of Digital Marketing

Digital marketing encompasses all the online activities you undertake to promote your music and brand. It includes everything from social media posts and email newsletters to paid advertising and content marketing. Understanding the fundamentals of digital marketing is crucial for creating a strategy that aligns with your goals and helps you achieve success.

8.1.1 Setting Clear Goals

Before diving into digital marketing, it's important to define what you want to achieve. Your goals will guide your strategy and help you measure success.

Common Digital Marketing Goals:

- **Growing Your Fanbase:** Expanding your audience by reaching new listeners and converting them into loyal fans.

- **Increasing Engagement:** Building a deeper connection with your existing audience through consistent interaction and communication.

- **Boosting Music Sales:** Driving more sales of your music, whether through digital downloads, streaming, or physical merchandise.

- **Promoting Live Events:** Increasing ticket sales and attendance at your live performances, tours, or virtual concerts.

- **Enhancing Brand Awareness:** Making your brand more recognizable and memorable to a broader audience.

8.1.2 Understanding Your Audience

Knowing your audience is the cornerstone of any effective digital marketing strategy. You need to understand who your fans are, what they care about, and how they interact with your music.

Steps to Understand Your Audience:

- **Demographics:** Gather information about your audience's age, gender, location, and other demographic factors.

- **Interests:** Identify what your audience is interested in beyond your music. This could include other artists they listen to, hobbies, and lifestyle preferences.

- **Behavior:** Analyze how your audience interacts with your content. When do they engage with your posts? What type of content do they prefer? How do they discover new music?

8.1.3 Creating a Content Strategy

Content is the lifeblood of digital marketing. Your content strategy should align with your goals and provide value to your audience while promoting your music and brand.

Types of Content to Consider:

● **Music Releases:** Share your music, whether it's a new single, album, or remix. Use platforms like SoundCloud, Spotify, and YouTube to reach your audience.

● **Behind-the-Scenes:** Give fans a glimpse into your creative process, whether it's writing lyrics, recording in the studio, or preparing for a live performance.

● **Live Performances:** Stream live performances, whether they're full concerts, acoustic sessions, or intimate performances.

● **Interviews and Collaborations:** Share interviews with you or collaborations with other artists. This content can provide insights into your personality and artistic journey.

● **Fan Interaction:** Create content that encourages fan participation, such as Q&A sessions, polls, and fan-generated content.

8.2 Building a Strong Online Presence

Your online presence is the foundation of your digital marketing efforts. It's where fans discover your music, learn about your brand, and interact with you.

MONETIZING YOUR MUSIC COPYRIGHTS AND BEYOND

8.2.1 Optimizing Your Website

Your website is your digital home base. It should be a comprehensive hub for all your content, including music, videos, tour dates, merchandise, and more.

Key Elements of an Effective Website:

● **Homepage:** Your homepage should immediately convey your brand and what you offer. Include a brief bio, a featured video or music player, and links to your social media profiles.

● **Music Page:** Dedicate a page to your music, where fans can listen, download, and stream your tracks. Include links to platforms like Spotify, Apple Music, and Bandcamp.

● **Tour and Events Page:** Keep your audience updated on upcoming live performances, tours, and virtual concerts. Include dates, locations, and ticket purchase links.

● **Store:** If you're selling merchandise, your website should have an easy-to-navigate store. Offer products like physical albums, T-shirts, posters, and other branded items.

● **Blog or News Section:** Use this space to share updates, news, and stories related to your music and career.

8.2.2 Leveraging Social Media

Social media platforms are powerful tools for connecting with your audience and promoting your music. Each platform has its strengths, and your strategy should reflect how your audience uses each one.

Popular Social Media Platforms for Musicians:

● **Instagram:** Ideal for visual content like photos, videos, and Stories. Use Instagram to showcase your lifestyle, share behind-the-scenes moments, and engage with fans.

- **Facebook:** Useful for building a community, sharing events, and posting longer-form content. Facebook Groups can be a great way to interact directly with your most loyal fans.

- **Twitter:** A platform for real-time interaction. Use Twitter for quick updates, engaging in conversations, and participating in trending topics.

- **TikTok:** Perfect for short-form video content. Use TikTok to create viral moments, share snippets of your music, and engage with trends.

- **YouTube:** The go-to platform for video content. Use YouTube to share music videos, live performances, vlogs, and other long-form content.

Tips for Social Media Success:

- **Consistency:** Post regularly to keep your audience engaged. Develop a content calendar to plan your posts in advance.

- **Engagement:** Respond to comments, like fan posts, and participate in conversations. Engagement is key to building a loyal community.

- **Authenticity:** Be authentic and true to your brand. Fans appreciate genuine interactions and content that reflects who you are as an artist.

- **Analytics:** Use social media analytics tools to track your performance. Analyze which posts perform best, what time of day your audience is most active, and how your follower count is growing.

8.2.3 Utilizing Email Marketing

Email marketing is a direct way to communicate with your fans and keep them informed about your latest releases, events, and news.

Creating an Effective Email Campaign:

● **Build Your List:** Start by building an email list of your fans. Offer a free download, exclusive content, or early access to tickets in exchange for their email address.

● **Segment Your Audience:** Segment your email list based on factors like location, fan engagement, and purchase history. This allows you to send more targeted and relevant content.

● **Personalize Your Emails:** Use the recipient's name and tailor the content to their interests. Personalized emails have higher open and click-through rates.

● **Design Engaging Emails:** Make sure your emails are visually appealing and easy to read. Include images, videos, and links to your latest content.

● **Track Performance:** Use email marketing tools to track metrics like open rates, click-through rates, and conversions. Use this data to refine your strategy and improve future campaigns.

8.3 Paid Advertising and Promotion

While organic reach is valuable, paid advertising can help you reach a wider audience and achieve your goals more quickly. Digital advertising offers precise targeting options that allow you to reach the right people at the right time.

8.3.1 Social Media Advertising

Social media platforms offer robust advertising options that allow you to target specific demographics, interests, and behaviors.

Popular Social Media Ad Formats:

- **Facebook and Instagram Ads:** Use Facebook Ads Manager to create campaigns across Facebook and Instagram. Choose from ad formats like image ads, video ads, carousel ads, and Stories ads.

- **YouTube Ads:** Promote your music videos or channel through YouTube ads. Options include skippable in-stream ads, non-skippable ads, and display ads.

- **TikTok Ads:** Use TikTok's ad platform to create short-form video ads that reach a younger, trend-focused audience.

Tips for Effective Social Media Advertising:

- **Targeting:** Use precise targeting to reach your ideal audience. Experiment with different audience segments to see what works best.

- **Creative:** Ensure your ad creative is eye-catching and aligned with your brand. Use high-quality images or videos and include a clear call to action.

- **Budgeting:** Start with a small budget and test different ads to see which perform best. Gradually increase your budget for ads that drive the most engagement and conversions.

- **Tracking:** Monitor your ad performance using platform analytics. Track key metrics like click-through rate (CTR), cost per click (CPC), and return on ad spend (ROAS).

8.3.2 Google Ads and Search Engine Marketing

Google Ads allows you to reach potential fans through search engine marketing (SEM). This is particularly useful for promoting your website, music, and merch.

Using Google Ads Effectively:

● **Keyword Research:** Identify relevant keywords that your target audience is likely to search for. Use tools like Google Keyword Planner to find the best keywords.

● **Ad Copy:** Write compelling ad copy that includes your target keywords and a clear call to action. Your ad should entice users to click through to your website or landing page.

● **Landing Pages:** Ensure that the landing page your ad directs to is optimized for conversions. It should be relevant to the ad, easy to navigate, and include a clear call to action.

● **Tracking and Optimization:** Use Google Analytics to track the performance of your ads. Optimize your campaigns based on metrics like CTR, conversion rate, and cost per acquisition (CPA).

8.4 Analytics and Optimization

Digital marketing is an ongoing process that requires regular analysis and optimization. Understanding your analytics is key to refining your strategy and improving your results.

8.4.1 Tracking Key Metrics

Identify the key metrics that align with your goals and track them consistently.

Common Digital Marketing Metrics:

● **Website Traffic:** The number of visitors to your website. Use Google Analytics to track traffic sources, bounce rate, and session duration.

● **Social Media Engagement:** Track likes, comments, shares, and follower growth on your social media platforms.

● **Email Marketing Metrics:** Monitor open rates, click-through rates, and unsubscribe rates to gauge the effectiveness of your email campaigns.

● **Ad Performance:** Track metrics like CTR, CPC, CPA, and ROAS to assess the effectiveness of your paid advertising campaigns.

● **Music Streams and Sales:** Track how your digital marketing efforts impact your music streams and sales on platforms like Spotify, Apple Music, and Bandcamp.

8.4.2 A/B Testing

A/B testing involves comparing two versions of a piece of content to see which performs better. This can be applied to everything from social media posts and email subject lines to ad copy and website landing pages.

Steps for Effective A/B Testing:

● **Identify a Variable:** Choose a single variable to test, such as the wording of a call to action, the image used in an ad, or the subject line of an email.

● **Create Variations:** Create two versions of the content with only the chosen variable changed.

● **Run the Test:** Split your audience into two groups and show each group one version of the content.

● **Analyze Results:** Compare the performance of each version based on your chosen metrics. Use the insights to inform future content decisions.

8.4.3 Continuous Improvement

Digital marketing is constantly evolving, and your strategy should too. Regularly review your performance, stay updated on industry trends, and be willing to adapt your approach as needed.

Conclusion

Digital marketing is a powerful tool for monetizing your music and growing your brand. By understanding the fundamentals, building a strong online presence, leveraging social media and email marketing, and optimizing your efforts through analytics, you can create a successful digital marketing strategy that drives your music career forward.

In the next chapter, we will explore the various ways to monetize your music through streaming platforms, sync licensing, and other digital revenue streams. We'll provide insights on how to maximize your earnings and protect your intellectual property in the digital landscape.

Chapter 9: Monetizing Your Music Through Streaming and Digital Platforms

In today's music industry, streaming and digital platforms have become the primary way audiences consume music. For independent artists, songwriters, publishers, and record labels, understanding how to effectively monetize music through these channels is essential for building a sustainable career. This chapter will delve into the various ways you can earn revenue from streaming platforms, optimize your digital presence, and leverage additional digital revenue streams.

9.1 The Streaming Economy: An Overview

Streaming has revolutionized the way music is distributed and consumed. Platforms like Spotify, Apple Music, YouTube, and Amazon Music have millions of users worldwide, offering artists a global reach. However, the streaming economy operates on a different model compared to traditional music sales, with revenue primarily generated through royalties.

9.1.1 How Streaming Royalties Work

Streaming royalties are typically divided into two categories: recording royalties and publishing royalties.

- **Recording Royalties:** These are paid to the owner of the master recording, often the record label or the artist if they own the masters.

- **Publishing Royalties:** These are paid to the songwriter and publisher for the composition. This includes performance royalties (for public performances or broadcasts) and mechanical royalties (for reproductions of the song).

Revenue per Stream: Streaming platforms pay artists a fraction of a cent per stream. The exact amount can vary based on factors such as the platform, country, and whether the listener is using a free or premium account. Understanding these dynamics is crucial for setting realistic financial expectations from streaming.

Payout Process:

● **Platform Royalties:** Streaming platforms collect revenue from subscriptions and ads, which are then distributed to rights holders based on stream counts.

● **Collection Societies and CMOs:** Performance royalties are collected by collection societies (CMOs), such as ASCAP, BMI, PRS, SAMRO, and others, depending on your country of registration.

● **Direct Payments:** Some platforms offer direct payments to artists for streaming revenue, while others distribute payments through record labels or aggregators.

9.1.2 Key Streaming Platforms

Different platforms cater to different audiences and offer unique opportunities for monetization.

Major Streaming Platforms:

● **Spotify:** With its massive user base, Spotify offers artists exposure and opportunities to be featured in curated playlists, which can significantly boost streams.

- **Apple Music:** Known for its high-quality streaming and curated playlists, Apple Music is a strong platform for artists who prioritize sound quality and brand alignment.

- **YouTube:** Beyond music videos, YouTube offers revenue through ad-supported content and premium subscriptions. Artists can also use YouTube's Content ID system to earn revenue from user-generated content.

- **Amazon Music:** This platform is growing rapidly, with a focus on integrating with Amazon's broader ecosystem, including smart speakers and e-commerce.

- **Tidal:** Known for its high payout rates and artist-centric approach, Tidal is a platform that offers higher royalties compared to many competitors.

Emerging and Niche Platforms:

- **Bandcamp:** While not a streaming platform per se, Bandcamp allows artists to sell digital downloads and physical merchandise directly to fans, often with a more artist-friendly revenue split.

- **SoundCloud:** Offers both streaming and direct fan support options, making it a hybrid platform for independent artists.

- **Deezer:** Popular in Europe, Deezer offers a unique user experience with its Flow feature, which helps users discover new music.

9.2 Maximizing Your Earnings on Streaming Platforms

To maximize your earnings from streaming, it's important to optimize your presence on each platform, engage with your audience, and understand how to leverage platform-specific features.

9.2.1 Optimizing Your Artist Profile

Your artist profile is the first impression potential fans get of you on streaming platforms. A well-optimized profile can help you attract more listeners and increase your streams.

Key Elements of an Optimized Profile:

● **Artist Bio:** Write a compelling and concise bio that tells your story. Highlight your achievements, influences, and what makes your music unique.

● **High-Quality Images:** Use professional, high-resolution images for your profile and cover photos. Consistency across platforms helps build brand recognition.

● **Links and Social Media:** Include links to your website, social media profiles, and other important platforms where fans can follow you and purchase your music.

● **Discography:** Ensure your entire discography is available and organized. Keep track of releases to ensure all your music is available on every platform.

● **Playlists:** Curate your own playlists or seek inclusion in popular ones. Playlists are a powerful tool for discovery and can significantly boost your streams.

9.2.2 Engaging with Your Audience

Engagement is key to growing your streaming numbers. The more you interact with your audience, the more likely they are to stream your music and share it with others.

Strategies for Audience Engagement:

- **Social Media Integration:** Promote your streaming links across your social media channels. Use features like Instagram Stories' music stickers or Twitter's share buttons to make it easy for fans to listen.

- **Live Streaming and Q&A Sessions:** Host live sessions where you perform, discuss your music, or answer fan questions. These interactions can drive more streams and deepen your connection with your audience.

- **Exclusive Content:** Offer exclusive content to your fans, such as early releases, behind-the-scenes footage, or bonus tracks. Platforms like Spotify allow artists to provide exclusive content to their followers.

- **Collaborations:** Collaborate with other artists to reach new audiences. Featuring on another artist's track or co-releasing music can expand your fan base and increase streams.

9.2.3 Leveraging Playlists

Playlists are one of the most effective ways to gain exposure on streaming platforms. Getting your music featured in popular playlists can lead to a significant increase in streams.

Types of Playlists:

- **Editorial Playlists:** Curated by platform editors, these playlists often have large followings and can provide substantial exposure. Submit your music to editors for consideration.

- **Algorithmic Playlists:** These are generated based on listener behavior. Examples include Spotify's Discover Weekly and Release Radar. Focus on building engagement to increase your chances of being featured.

● **User-Generated Playlists:** These are created by individual users or influencers. Engaging with playlist curators and fans can help get your music included in these lists.

Tips for Playlist Inclusion:

● **Pitching Your Music:** Use platform tools to pitch your music for playlist inclusion. Be concise and highlight why your track fits the playlist's theme or mood.

● **Building Relationships:** Network with playlist curators, influencers, and other artists to increase your chances of being featured.

● **Consistency:** Regularly release new music to keep your presence fresh and increase your chances of playlist inclusion.

9.3 Beyond Streaming: Other Digital Revenue Streams

In addition to streaming, there are several other digital revenue streams available to independent artists. These can provide additional income and help diversify your revenue sources.

9.3.1 Digital Downloads

Although streaming has largely replaced digital downloads, there is still a market for high-quality downloads, particularly among dedicated fans.

Platforms for Digital Downloads:

● **Bandcamp:** Allows artists to sell digital downloads directly to fans, often with a higher revenue split than other platforms.

● **iTunes/Apple Music:** Despite the rise of streaming, iTunes remains a popular platform for purchasing music, especially in album format.

MONETIZING YOUR MUSIC COPYRIGHTS AND BEYOND

- **Amazon:** Offers both physical and digital sales, providing another avenue for fans to purchase your music.

Strategies for Maximizing Digital Downloads:

- **Exclusive Content:** Offer exclusive tracks, remixes, or live recordings as digital downloads to incentivize purchases.

- **Bundling:** Create bundles that include digital downloads along with merchandise or physical copies of your music.

- **Direct Sales:** Promote your digital downloads directly to your email list and social media followers, emphasizing the benefits of owning your music.

9.3.2 Sync Licensing

Sync licensing involves placing your music in films, TV shows, commercials, video games, and other media. This can be a lucrative revenue stream and provides significant exposure.

How Sync Licensing Works:

- **Licensing Agreements:** A sync license grants the rights to use your music in a specific media project. This is usually negotiated by your publisher or a sync agency.

- **Revenue:** Sync deals can be highly lucrative, with upfront payments and potential royalties from the media project's distribution.

Strategies for Getting Sync Placements:

- **Catalog and Metadata:** Ensure your music catalog is organized and includes detailed metadata. This makes it easier for music supervisors to find and license your tracks.

- **Networking:** Build relationships with music supervisors, sync agencies, and other industry professionals who work in media production.

- **Tailoring Your Music:** Create tracks that fit common sync themes, such as emotional moments, action scenes, or commercial jingles.

9.3.3 YouTube and Content ID

YouTube offers multiple ways to monetize your music, including through ads, Content ID, and fan support.

Monetization Options on YouTube:

- **Ads:** Enable monetization on your videos to earn revenue from ads. The amount you earn depends on factors like views, ad engagement, and your audience's location.

- **Content ID:** YouTube's Content ID system scans videos for your music and allows you to monetize user-generated content that includes your tracks.

- **Channel Memberships and Super Chat:** Engage directly with your fans through YouTube's membership and Super Chat features, allowing fans to support you financially.

Tips for Maximizing YouTube Revenue:

- **Optimize Your Channel:** Ensure your YouTube channel is fully optimized with an engaging profile, clear branding, and playlists that encourage long watch times.

- **Consistent Uploads:** Regularly upload content to keep your audience engaged and increase your chances of earning revenue from ads and Content ID.

- **Engage with Your Community:** Respond to comments, host live chats, and create content that encourages interaction and sharing.

9.3.4 Crowdfunding and Fan Support

Crowdfunding platforms and direct fan support can provide additional revenue streams, especially for independent artists who have a dedicated fan base.

Popular Crowdfunding Platforms:

● **Patreon:** Allows fans to support you on a recurring basis in exchange for exclusive content and perks.

● **Kickstarter/Indiegogo:** Use these platforms to fund specific projects, such as album production, tours, or music videos.

● **Bandcamp:** In addition to selling music, Bandcamp offers options for fans to support you directly through donations or special releases.

Strategies for Successful Crowdfunding:

● **Clear Goals:** Set clear, achievable goals for your crowdfunding campaigns. Explain how the funds will be used and what backers will receive in return.

● **Engaging Content:** Create compelling content to promote your campaign, including videos, updates, and personal messages.

● **Exclusive Rewards:** Offer unique rewards to incentivize backers, such as limited edition merchandise, exclusive tracks, or personalized experiences.

Conclusion

Monetizing your music through streaming and digital platforms requires a strategic approach. By optimizing your presence on streaming services, engaging with your audience, and exploring additional digital revenue streams, you can build a sustainable income from your music. Remember, success in the digital age involves continuous learning and adaptation, so stay informed about industry trends and be open to experimenting with new strategies.

In the next chapter, we will explore the importance of building a strong live performance strategy and how touring, live shows, and virtual concerts can enhance your music career and increase your revenue streams. We'll also discuss the logistics of organizing tours and the financial aspects of live performances.

Chapter 10: Conclusion

Crafting Your Unique Monetization Strategy

As you reach the end of this guide, it's crucial to remember that the journey of monetizing your music copyrights is deeply personal and unique to each artist, songwriter, and entrepreneur. There isn't a one-size-fits-all approach. Your strategy will depend on your goals, your music, your audience, and the resources available to you.

To craft your own strategy, start by evaluating where you are in your career and where you want to go. Are you an independent artist looking to build a sustainable income stream, or are you a songwriter aiming to maximize royalties from compositions? Perhaps you're a music entrepreneur seeking to expand your catalog's reach internationally. Understanding your specific objectives will help you prioritize the steps you need to take.

Next, consider the various revenue streams available to you, as discussed throughout this book. Whether it's maximizing royalties, exploring synchronization deals, leveraging digital platforms, or diving into emerging opportunities like NFTs and blockchain, each revenue stream offers different benefits and challenges. Choose the ones that align with your strengths and aspirations.

Finally, continuously refine your approach. The music industry is dynamic, and what works today may not work tomorrow. Regularly assess your strategy, track your results, and be willing to pivot when necessary. Stay informed about industry trends, new technologies, and evolving legal frameworks to ensure that your strategy remains effective and relevant.

The Importance of Adaptability in the Modern Music Industry

Adaptability is the key to long-term success in the music industry. As we've seen throughout this book, the industry is constantly evolving, driven by technological advancements, changes in consumer behavior, and shifts in the global marketplace. To thrive, you must be willing to adapt—not just to survive but to take advantage of new opportunities as they arise.

Embrace the idea that learning never stops. Stay curious, seek out new information, and don't be afraid to experiment with different approaches. Whether it's testing a new social media platform, exploring alternative revenue streams, or collaborating with international partners, your ability to adapt and innovate will set you apart from others in the industry.

Building a successful music career is a marathon, not a sprint. Patience, perseverance, and a willingness to learn from both successes and failures will serve you well.

Next Steps: Implementing What You've Learned

Now that you've absorbed the knowledge and insights from this book, it's time to take action. Here are some practical steps to help you get started:

1. **Conduct a Self-Assessment**: Reflect on your current position in the music industry. What are your strengths? Where do you see opportunities for growth? Identify any gaps in your knowledge or resources and make a plan to address them.
2. **Set Clear Goals**: Define what success looks like for you. Whether it's earning a specific amount of royalties, securing a high-profile synchronization deal, or building a global

fanbase, having clear, measurable goals will guide your efforts.

3. **Create a Monetization Plan**: Based on the strategies discussed in this book, outline a plan that includes the revenue streams you want to focus on, the platforms and tools you'll use, and the timelines for achieving your goals.

4. **Build Your Team**: Identify the key team members you need to support your journey, whether it's a manager, booking agent, publicist, or a music business consultant. Consider your budget and the specific expertise each role brings to the table.

5. **Start Small and Scale**: Begin by implementing one or two strategies from your plan, focusing on areas where you can make the most immediate impact. As you gain experience and momentum, gradually scale up your efforts to include additional revenue streams and markets.

6. **Monitor and Adjust**: Regularly review your progress, track your income streams, and assess the effectiveness of your strategies. Be prepared to adjust your plan as needed to respond to new challenges and opportunities.

Embrace the Journey

The path to monetizing your music copyrights and building a successful career is filled with both challenges and rewards. It requires dedication, creativity, and a proactive approach. But with the right mindset, the strategies outlined in this book, and a commitment to continuous learning, you can achieve your goals and create a sustainable and profitable music career.

Remember, success in the music mkidustry isn't just about the money—it's about creating something meaningful that resonates with audiences, both locally and globally. As you move forward, keep your passion for music at the forefront, and let that drive your efforts to share your art with the world.

Thank you for taking the time to explore these insights and strategies. The music industry is waiting for you to make your mark. Now it's your turn to take what you've learned and turn it into action.

Next Steps:

● Review the sample contracts and agreements in the appendices.

● Reach out to the global CMOs and resources listed to begin your registration process.

● Stay connected with the music community and industry news to keep up with emerging trends.

● Most importantly, start implementing your monetization strategy today.

Good luck, and here's to your success in monetizing your music copyrights and beyond!

Glossary of Music Industry Terms

---

1. Advance: A lump sum payment given to an artist or songwriter before royalties are earned, typically recoupable against future earnings.

2. Backend Royalties: Earnings generated after the initial advance has been recouped by the record label or publisher.

3. Copyright: The legal right granted to the creator of an original work, protecting the use and distribution of that work.

4. Mechanical Royalties: Payments to songwriters and publishers for the reproduction of their music, such as in CDs, vinyl, or digital downloads.

**5. Performance Royalties: Payments made to songwriters, composers, and publishers when their music is performed publicly, such as on the radio, TV, or live venues.

**6. Synchronization License: A license granting the right to use music in visual media, such as films, TV shows, or commercials.

**7. Publishing Agreement: A contract between a songwriter and a music publisher outlining the rights and revenue shares for the use of the songwriter's works.

**8. Distribution Agreement: A contract between an artist or label and a distributor, detailing the terms for distributing music to the public.

**9. Collective Management Organization (CMO): An organization that administers the rights and royalties of artists and songwriters on their behalf.

**10. Digital Aggregator: A service that distributes music to digital platforms, such as streaming services and online stores, on behalf of artists and labels.

Don't miss out!

Visit the website below and you can sign up to receive emails whenever Thando Mkize publishes a new book. There's no charge and no obligation.

https://books2read.com/r/B-A-QIOIC-ROJWE

BOOKS2READ

Connecting independent readers to independent writers.

About the Author

Thando Mkize is an accomplished music business consultant, digital marketer, and social media manager with a rich background in the music industry. As the founder of Agapelove Consultancy, Thando has dedicated his career to empowering independent artists, music industry practitioners, and businesses by providing innovative and tailored consultancy services. His expertise spans across copyright administration, licensing, and music business law, honed through his previous roles at Sheer Publishing Africa and CAPASSO.

Thando's journey into the music business began in 2017 while studying Music Business Law, Contracts, and Copyrights at the Academy of Sound Engineering. His passion for supporting artists through the often complex and challenging terrain of the music industry led him to write his latest book, which serves as a comprehensive guide for independent artists, songwriters, publishers, record labels, and music entrepreneurs looking to monetize their music copyrights and explore new revenue streams.

With a deep understanding of the global music landscape, Thando's book offers practical insights and strategies for setting up a successful, international music business. He continues to be a leading voice in the industry, advocating for the rights and success of independent artists worldwide.